FROM ZERO TO PRO

MW00901360

PHP and MySQL Programming for Beginners:

A Step by Step Course

By Matthew Gimson

Table of Contents

Part 1 - Introduction to PHP

PHP (Hypertext Preprocessor) is a server-side scripting language preferred by many web designers both for its straightforward language and its high level of security. The language is easy to learn even for beginners and is used by Android developers to link their apps with MySQL database. Content Management Systems such as Drupal, Joomla, and WordPress employ PHP as the language behind their development because of its powerful and easy interfacing with databases and computer operating systems alike.

The code for PHP can be written on any program which can handle a ".php" extension, giving a wide range of options for you to choose from. Many word processors such as Notepad or Notepad++ are suitable for PHP code writing. It should be noted, however that more specialized programs such as Adobe Dreamweaver, are recommended as they streamline the code writing process making the whole thing much simpler and faster.

PHP was created beginning in 1994 by Rasmus Lerdorf for the purpose of web development. He did this by employing Common Gateway Interface binaries written using the C programming language. Today, however, programmers also use it for more general-purpose programming and it can be combined with HTML to add functionality to the user interface of a web application, and this in addition to numerous other web frameworks and template engines. A *"PHP Interpreter"* is responsible for processing of PHP code, and it is usually implemented on the server side as a module. After the code has been interpreted the server sends the results to the client in the form of a web page.

First PHP Program

Now, let us begin by writing our first PHP program. Just open your text editor and write the following code:

```
<!DOCTYPE html>
<html>
<body>
<?php
echo "first PHP script!";
?>
</body>
</html>
```

After writing the program, save the file with a "*.php*" extension and then open it with your browser. You will observe the following output:

first PHP script!

Notice the placement of the text in the program which has formed this output.

Comments & PHP syntax

Comments are not processed by the interpreter. They are only made available to be read by the human programmer. There are two ways of denoting comments in PHP. The first way is the *"Single-Line"* comment, whereas the second way is the *"Block"* comment.

Single line comments are denoted using the pound sign (#). This is demonstrated in the example shown below:

```
<?
# This is the first line of comment
# This forms the second line of comments
// this is also a comment. Denotes a second way for
single-line commenting
print "A single-commenting example in PHP";
?>
```

Other than using the pound sign for single-line commenting, we can also use two forward slash symbols (//) for the same purpose. This can also be seen in the example above.

For block comments, or multi-line comments, we use other symbols. This is demonstrated in the following example:

```
<?
/* PHP (Hypertext Preprocessor) is a server-side
scripting language. It was developed for the purpose of
web development. However, programmers also use it
for general-purpose programming. */
print "A multi-line comment in PHP";
?>
```

HTML script tags take the following syntax in PHP:

```
<script language="PHP">...</script>
```

It is worth noting that PHP is case sensitive. Consider the following example:

```
<html>
<body>
<?php
$age = 30;
```

```
print("The age is $age<br>");
print("The age is $aGe<br>");
?>
</body>
</html>
```

Run the program by opening it in your browser. You will observe the following output:

```
The age is 30
The age is
PHP Notice: Undefined variable: aGe in /web/com/1430831286_17502/main.php on line 6
```

The error is due to the use of capital rather than lowercase "G" in the variable "*aGe*" rather than "*age*". The first line of the output is okay while the second line encounters an undefined variable.

PHP Variables

In PHP code, variables are used to store information and are written using a dollar sign ($). To assign a variable a value, we use the assignment operator (=).

PHP supports numerous variables including the following:

- **Integers**- these are whole numbers with no decimal point, example 2345.

- **Doubles**- these are floating-point numbers, example 4.7845 or 89.3.

- **Booleans**- can either be a true or a false.

- **NULL**- this is a special type and it takes only one value: NULL.

- **Strings**- made up of a sequence of characters, example "this is a string in PHP.'

- **Arrays**- they represent indices of other values. They are named.

- **Objects**- these are classes which have been defined by the programmer. They can be used to package both methods and attributes into a single entity.

- **Resources**- are a special type of variables used to represent external resources such as connection to the database.

Part 2 - Decision Making in PHP: Statements and Loops

With PHP, one can develop logic programs by use of the decision making statements. Let us discuss these statements.

The "if...else" Statement

Used for execution when a part of the code is true and the other one is false. It takes the following syntax:

if (expression)
code for execution once the condition is met (true);
else
code to be executed if the condition is not met (false);

Consider the following example:

```
<html>
<body>
<?php
```

```php
$grade=("B");
if ($grade=="B")
echo "You really tried, maintain!";
else
echo "will tell you later!";
?>
</body>
</html>
```

Save and run the program. It should output the following:

You really tried, maintain!

Consider what happens if we change the grade but maintain the other parts:

```php
<html>
<body>
<?php
$grade=("D");
if ($grade=="B")
echo "You really tried, maintain!";
else
echo "will tell you later!";
?>
```

```html
</body>
</html>
```

This will give the following result:

will tell you later!

In our first program, the condition in the "*if*" statement has been met, so the first "*echo*" statement is executed. In our second program, the condition in the "*else*" statement was the one met, so the second "*echo*" statement is executed. This shows how simple it is to use this statement.

If you need to execute more than one line once the condition is met or not met, then curly brackets ({}), also called braces, should be used to enclose these statements.

This is demonstrated in the following example:

```
<html>
<body>
<?php
$grade=("B");
if ($grade=="B")
{
```

```php
echo "Hello!<br />";
echo "You really tried!";
echo "maintain it and you will see a difference";
}
?>
</body>
</html>
```

The "else...if" Statement

This is normally used when there are several conditions to be met. It takes the following syntax:

if (condition)
statement to be executed if condition is met (true);
elseif (condition)
statement to be executed if condition is met (true);
else
statement to be executed if condition is not met (false);

Consider the following example:

```
<html>
<body>
<?php
$grade=("B");
if ($grade=="B")
echo "You really tried, maintain!";
elseif ($grade=="C")
echo "That is fair, you can improve!";
else
```

```php
        echo "unknown grade!";
        ?>
        </body>
        </html>
```

Again, write this program, save and then open it with your browser.

You will observe the following output:

You reallytried, maintain!

The output shows that the condition in the "*if*" statement was met. Let us try to change the grade:

```php
        <html>
        <body>
        <?php
        $grade=("C");
        if ($grade=="B")
      echo "You really tried, maintain!";
        elseif ($grade=="C")
      echo "That is fair, you can improve!";
```

```
                        else
              echo "unknown grade!";
                        ?>
                     </body>
                     </html>
```

The above program will give the following output:

That is fair, you can improve!

Notice that this time, we have set the grade to "*C*". From the output, it is clear that the condition in the "*elseif*" statement was met. Finally, let us try to change the grade so as to meet the final condition:

```
                    <html>
                    <body>
                    <?php
                 $grade=("F");
                if ($grade=="B")
          echo "You really tried, maintain!";
```

```
        elseif ($grade=="C")
    echo "That is fair, you can improve!";
               else
        echo "unknown grade!";
                 ?>
              </body>
              </html>
```

Notice that we have changed the grade to "*F*" which we have not defined. The program will give the following output:

unkwown grade!

The output shows that neither of the first two conditions was met.

The "switch" Statement

If one or more blocks of code need to be selected for execution, then use this statement. It can also be used to substitute the "*if...else*" statement. It takes the following syntax:

switch (expression)
{
case condition1:
statement to be executed if "*condition1*" is true;
break;
case condition2:
statement to be executed if "*condition2*" is true;
break;
default:
statement to be executed if "*condition 1*" and
"*condition2*" are different from the expression;
}

Consider the example given below:

<html>
<body>
<?php

```
$grade=("B");
switch ($grade)
{
case "A":
echo "that is excellent";
break;
case "B":
echo "That is good";
break;
case "C":
echo "That is a fair";
break;
case "D":
echo "This is poor. You must work hard";
break;
case "E":
echo "This is failure. Repeat";
break;
case "F":
echo "You are discontinued";
break;
case "X":
echo "never did the exam";
break;
default:
```

```php
      echo "unknown results.";
   }
?>
</body>
</html>
```

After running the above program, you will get the following output:

That is good

If none of the conditions had been met, the default statement would have been executed. However the output above shows that the grade is "B". Let us now change the grade to an undefined one:

```php
<html>
<body>
<?php
$grade=("G");
switch ($grade)
{
case "A":
```

```php
    echo "that is excellent";
    break;
case "B":
    echo "That is good";
    break;
case "C":
    echo "That is a fair";
    break;
case "D":
    echo "This is poor. You must work hard";
    break;
case "E":
    echo "This is failure. Repeat";
    break;
case "F":
    echo "You are discontinued";
    break;
case "X":
    echo "never did the exam";
    break;
default:
    echo "unknown results.";
}
?>
</body>
```

</html>

The grade "*G*" has not been defined in our case statements. This leads to the following output:

unknown results.

Loops in PHP

In PHP, loops are used when a part of the code needs to be executed a certain number of times. A condition is set and as long as the condition is met, then the loop will continue to execute. Execution will only stop when the condition is no longer satisfied. In this section we are going to discuss some of the loops supported in PHP.

The "for" Loop

This is used if the number of times that a statement or a block of statements is to be executed is known. It takes the following syntax:

for (initial value; condition; increment)
{
code for execution if condition is met;
}

The initial value is the number at which the counter begins and the condition sets the minimum and the maximum number of times that the code is to be executed.

You can choose to declare a variable in the loop.

Consider the following example:

```
<html>
<body>
<?php
$x = 0;
$y = 0;

for( $j=0; $j<5; $j++ )
{
$x += 1;
$y += 2;
}
echo (" x=$x and y=$y" );
?>
</body>
</html>
```

Just write the program as it is above, save, and then open it in your browser. You will observe the following output:

x=5 and y=10

We have two variables, "x" and "y", both have been initialized at zero (0), undergo 5 iterations. "x" increases by 1 with each iteration whereas "y" increases by 2. This explains how we get the above result. Once the 5 iterations have been completed, the loop will stop executing since if it continues, it will violate the condition set in the loop.

The "while" Loop

This loop will continue to execute as long as the specified condition is satisfied. Testing of the condition will continue as long as the execution is in progress. Once the condition is found to be false, however, execution of the loop will end. It takes the following syntax:

while (expression)

{

Code for execution if the expression is true;

}

Consider the example given below:

<html>

<body>

<?php

$j = 0;

$value = 20;

while($j < 10)

{

$value--;

$j++;

}

```php
echo ("The final value of the variables is:  j = $j and
value = $value" );
?>
</body>
</html>
```

Write the program and then save it. Open it in your browser and you will get the following output:

The final value of the variables is: j = 10 and value = 10

We have started by initializing the values for our two variables, "*j*" and "*value*". Variable "*j*" will count the number of times that the variable "*value*" is decreased. In each iteration, the value of the variable is decreased by 1. At the same time, the value of variable "*j*" is increased by 1. Once "*j*" increases 10 times, the loop will stop executing. This explains the source of the output in the above figure.

The "do...while" Loop

In this loop, even if the test condition is not met, the loop must be executed at least once. The test condition is usually placed at the end, and it will always be executed as long as the test condition is true.

It takes the following syntax:

```
do
{
Code to be executed if condition is true;
}while (condition);
```

Consider the following example:

```
<html>
<body>
<?php
$j = 0;do{
$j++;
}while( $j < 10 );
echo ("Final value of j is: $j" );
?>
</body>
</html>
```

Run the program and you will observe the following output:

Final value of j is: 10

What happens is that we initialize the value of "j" at zero (0)? This value is increased by 1 with each iteration until it reaches 10. This marks the point where the loop ends.

The "foreach" Loop

Used for looping through arrays. For each iteration made, the current element of the array is assigned to $value. The pointer of the array is also moved to the next element of the array. It takes the following syntax:

foreach (array as a value)

{

Code for execution;

}

Consider the following example:

```
<html>
<body>
<?php
$myarray = array( a, b, c, d, e);
foreach( $myarray as $value )
{
echo "The letter is $value <br />";
}
```

```
?>
</body>
</html>
```

Write the above program, save and then run it. You will observe the following output:

The letter is a
The letter is b
The letter is c
The letter is d
The letter is e

The "break" Statement

This is used to prematurely halt the execution of a loop. With this statement, you can exercise full control of the loop. Once you are out of the loop, you can then execute its immediate statement. Consider the following example:

```
<html>
<body>
<?php
$j = 0;
while( $j < 10)
    {
    $j++;
    if( $j == 5 )break;
    }
echo (" The Loop stopped at j = $j" );
?>
</body>
</html>
```

Write the program and then run it. The following output will be observed:

$$\text{The Loop stopped at } j = 5$$

In the "*if*" statement, we have instructed the loop to break once it finds that the value of "*j*" is 5. This explains the source of the output.

The "continue" statement

This statement is used to end the current iteration of a loop without terminating it. This is done by placing it inside the block of statements that the loop executes. It is preceded by the conditional test. Consider the following example:

```
<html>
<body>
<?php
$myarray = array( a, b, c, d, e);
foreach( $myarray as $value )
{
if( $value == c )continue;
echo "The letter is $value <br />";
}
?>
</body>
</html>
```

Run the program and observe the result. The following should be the output:

The letter is a
The letter is b
The letter is d
The letter is e

As you can see, the value "c" is not part of the output. When the interpreter finds that the value to be printed is "c", it skips that value and then the next element of the array is processed. This explains the source of the above output.

Get & Post Methods

The client has two methods to send information to the server:

- GET Method
- POST Method

Before the browser sends the information to the server, it must encode it using a method called *"URL encoding"*.

"GET" method

This method is used to send the messages or details to an encoded user. A "*?*" is used to separate the encoded information and the page as shown below:

http://www.sample.com/index.htm?firstname=value1& secondname=value2

Consider the example given below:

```php
<?php
if( $_GET["username"] || $_GET["age"] )
{
echo "You are ". $_GET['username']. "<br />";
echo "Your age is ". $_GET['age']. " years old.";
exit();
}
```

```
                    ?>

                  <html>

                  <body>

<form action="<?php $_PHP_SELF ?>"
            method="GET">

UserName: <input type="text" name="username" />

Age: <input type="text" name="age" />

<input type="submit" value="Submit"/>

                  </form>

                  </body>

                  </html>
```

Just write this program, save and then open it with your browser. You will observe the following output:

UserName: [   ] Age: [   ] Submit

You can provide your details just as you have been directed. Once you are done, click on the *"Submit"* button and observe what happens.

Part 3 - Working with the Database

MySQL is the most widely used relational SQL database management system and is commonly used with the development of web applications. It is an open source software available for free download either through MySQL itself or through "WampServer".

After installing, open the MySQL command prompt. This can either be accessed through the start menu or you can just search for "*mysql*". If you are using WampServer, make sure that it is running then click on the triangular icon in the task bar, on the bottom right corner of your screen. From there you can access the program by clicking on the WampServer and then MySQL-> MySQL console. If you have already created a password during installation use that same password on the command prompt which will appear.

Connecting to MySQL

To connect to MySQL from PHP, we use the function *"mysql_connect()"*. The function takes five parameters. This is shown in the syntax below:

connection

mysql_connect(server_name,username,password,new _link,client_flag);

The *"server_name"* is the name of the host where the database is running. If you don't specify this, then the default becomes *"localhost:3306"*. The *"username"* is the name of the user who is trying to access the database. If you don't specify this, then it will be set to the name of the user who owns the server process. If you have not set up a password during the installation process, leave this field blank. Otherwise, use the password you created.

To connect to your database, use the following code:

```php
<?php
$dbhost = 'localhost:3036';
$dbuser = 'root';
$dbpass = '';
$con = mysql_connect($dbhost, $dbuser, $dbpass);
if(! $conn )
{
die('Failed to connect: ' . mysql_error());
}
echo 'The connection was successful';
mysql_close($con);
?>
```

However, make sure that the database host or *"dbhost"*, database user or *"dbuser"* and database password or *"dbpass"* are set according to the settings of your own system. For my own system, I have connected to the database as the "root" user and I have not set any password for my database and that is why I have left the field for password blank in the example above.

Closing Connection to the Database

Once you are through with what you were doing with the MySQL database, it is important that you close it. Use the following PHP code to do so:

```php
<?php
$dbhost = 'localhost:3036';
$dbuser = 'root';
$dbpass = '';
$con = mysql_connect($dbhost, $dbuser, $dbpass);
if(! $con )
{
die('Failed to connect: ' . mysql_error());
}
echo 'Connection was successful';
mysql_close($con);
?>
```

Creating a new Database

In order to create a new database in MySQL with PHP you must have the admin privilege. We use the *"mysql_query"* function for this purpose. If the function succeeds, it returns a *"true"* response, but if it fails it returns a *"false"* response.

The function takes the following two parameters:

bool mysql_query(sql, connection);

The following is the description of the above two parameters:

- **Sql**- this must be specified. It is the SQL *query to create* a new database
- **Connection** – this must not be specified. If it is not specified, the last opened connection by *"mysql_connect"* is used.

Consider the code given below:

```php
<?php
$dbhost = 'localhost:3036';
$dbuser = 'root';
$dbpass = '';
$con = mysql_connect($dbhost, $dbuser, $dbpass);
if(! $con )
{
die('Failed to connect: ' . mysql_error());
}
echo 'Connection was successful';
$sql = 'CREATE Database mydb';
$rval = mysql_query( $sql, $con );
if(! $rval )
{
die('Failed to create the database: ' . mysql_error());
}
echo "The Database mydb was created successfully\n";
mysql_close($con);
?>
```

In the code above, I have executed a query to create a new MySQL database called *"mydb"*. Just write the program and then execute it by opening it with your browser to check whether the database has been created. In my case, I get the following output when I checked:

```
mysql> Show databases;
+--------------------+
| Database           |
+--------------------+
| information_schema |
| db                 |
| mydb               |
| mysql              |
| performance_schema |
| test               |
+--------------------+
6 rows in set (0.00 sec)
```

The above figure shows all the available databases on my computer. As you can see the new database which I just created is also available, meaning the program was successfully executed.

Now that you know how to create a new database in MySQL using PHP, you also need to know how to select the right database to work on. To do this, we use *"mysql_select_db"* function which takes the following syntax:

bool mysql_select_db(db_name, connection);

The method returns *"true"* after a successful selection and a *"false"* after a failed selection.

Consider the program code shown below:

```php
<?php
$dbhost = 'localhost:3036';
$dbuser = 'root';
$dbpass = '';
$con = mysql_connect($dbhost, $dbuser, $dbpass);
if(! $con )
{
die('Failed to connect: ' . mysql_error());
}
echo 'Connection was successful';
mysql_select_db( 'mydb' );
```

```
mysql_close($con);
?>
```

Make sure that you modify the connections according to your
settings before running the program, otherwise, you will get an
error.

Creating Tables

After connecting to MySQL and selecting the right database to work with, you might need to create a number of tables in the database, a task which can easily be achieved with PHP. To start, write the query responsible for creating the table and then execute it using the "*mysql_query()*" function. Consider the program given below:

```php
<?php
$dbhost = 'localhost:3036';
$dbuser = 'root';
$dbpass = '';
$con = mysql_connect($dbhost, $dbuser, $dbpass);
if(! $con )
{
die('Failed to connect: ' . mysql_error());
}
echo 'Connection was successful';
$sql = 'CREATE TABLE student(
'student_id INT NOT NULL AUTO_INCREMENT, '.
'student_name VARCHAR(20) NOT NULL, '.
'student_address  VARCHAR(20) NOT NULL, '.
```

```
            'student_age   INT NOT NULL, '.
          'join_date   timestamp(14) NOT NULL, '.
              'primary key ( student_id ))';
                mysql_select_db('mydb');
            $rval = mysql_query( $sql, $con );
                      if(! $rval )
                          {
        die('Failed to create the table: ' . mysql_error());
                          }
        echo "Table student was created successfully\n";
                  mysql_close($con);
                        ?>
```

After running the above program, check to see whether the table has been created. This is demonstrated in the following figure:

```
mysql> use mydb;
Database changed
mysql> show tables
    -> ;
+-----------------+
| Tables_in_mydb  |
+-----------------+
| students        |
+-----------------+
1 row in set (0.00 sec)

mysql>
```

This shows that the table has been created. You should also check its attributes (columns) to verify whether they are correct. This is illustrated in the following figure:

```
mysql> desc students;
+----------------+-------------+------+-----+---------+----------------+
| Field          | Type        | Null | Key | Default | Extra          |
+----------------+-------------+------+-----+---------+----------------+
| student_id     | int(11)     | NO   | PRI | NULL    | auto_increment |
| student_name   | varchar(20) | NO   |     | NULL    |                |
| student_address| varchar(20) | NO   |     | NULL    |                |
| student_age    | int(11)     | NO   |     | NULL    |                |
| join_date      | timestamp(6)| NO   |     | NULL    |                |
+----------------+-------------+------+-----+---------+----------------+
5 rows in set (0.03 sec)

mysql>
```

As you can see, the figure above shows that the table has, in fact, been formed with the attributes which we had specified.

It is also possible to create a text file with the parameters for your table. This text file should then be loaded into the PHP program. This is the easiest and quickest way to achieve this.

Create a text file with the following:

```
CREATE TABLE students(
student_id INT NOT NULL AUTO_INCREMENT,
student_name VARCHAR(20) NOT NULL,
student_address  VARCHAR(20) NOT NULL,
student_age   INT NOT NULL,
join_date   timestamp(14) NOT NULL,
primary key ( student_id ));
```

Save this text file with the name *"mytextfile.txt"* then write the following PHP program:

```php
<?php
$dbhost = 'localhost:3036';
$dbuser = 'root';
$dbpass = '';
$conn = mysql_connect($dbhost, $dbuser, $dbpass);
if(! $con )
{
die('Failed to connect: ' . mysql_error());
}
```

```php
$query_file = 'mytextfile.txt';

$fo   = fopen($query_file, 'r');
$sql = fread($fo, filesize($query_file));
fclose($fo);

mysql_select_db('mydb');
$rval = mysql_query( $sql, $con );
if(! $rval )
{
die('Failed to create table: ' . mysql_error());
}
echo "Table students ws  created successfully\n";
mysql_close($con);
?>
```

You can then run the program checking in with the database to see whether the table has been created. You should find that it has been created.

Deleting the database

Once you have set up a database, it may eventually be necessary to delete it. This can easily be achieved with PHP. All you have to do is create a query for this task and then execute it using the *"mysql_query()"* function.

This is illustrated by the program below:

```php
<?php
$dbhost = 'localhost:3036';
$dbuser = 'root';
$dbpass = '';
$con = mysql_connect($dbhost, $dbuser, $dbpass);
if(! $con )
{
die('Failed to connect: ' . mysql_error());
}
$sql = 'DROP DATABASE mydb';
$rval = mysql_query( $sql, $con );
if(! $rval )
{
die('Failed to delete database mydb: ' . mysql_error());
```

```
}
echo "The Database was deleted successfully\n";
mysql_close($con);
?>
```

Please be aware that once you have deleted your database you will lose everything contained in it. For this reason, be sure of your choice before running the above program.

Deleting a Table

Sometimes you might need to delete only a single table rather than deleting the whole database. PHP makes this work easy. All that is required is to create a query for this task and then execute it using the *"mysql_query"* function. Again, this should be done with a great deal of care as it is possible to lose very important information.

Consider the example given below:

```php
<?php
$dbhost = 'localhost:3036';
$dbuser = 'root';
$dbpass = '';
$con = mysql_connect($dbhost, $dbuser, $dbpass);
if(! $con )
{
die('Failed to connect: ' . mysql_error());
}
$sql = 'DROP TABLE students';
$rval = mysql_query( $sql, $con );
if(! $rval )
{
```

```
        die('Failed to delete the table students: ' .
                mysql_error());
        }
echo "The table  was deleted successfully\n";
            mysql_close($con);
                    ?>
```

Again, modify the conditions to fit your settings, including the name of the host, the username and the password. Once you run the above program, the table *"students"* will be deleted from the database, meaning that it will be no longer be accessible.

Inserting Data into a Database

Once you have created your database as well as your database table, you might need to insert some data into the table. The data you wish to insert may be specified inside the PHP code or you may choose to do this by creating an HTML form. An HTML form allows users to then enter the data themselves. PHP, on the other hand, should be used to get data from the HTML form transferred into the MySQL database. It is at this point that the value of PHP begins to present itself

Let us begin by illustrating the first and simplest method for doing this, specifying the data within the PHP code. Just write the following program:

```php
<?php
$dbhost = 'localhost:3036';
$dbuser = 'root';
$dbpass = '';
$conn = mysql_connect($dbhost, $dbuser, $dbpass);
if(! $con )
```

```php
{
die('Failed to connect: ' . mysql_error());
}
$sql = 'INSERT INTO students '.
'(student_name,student_address, student_age, join_date) '.
'VALUES ( "john", "HJK, 13, NOW() )';

mysql_select_db('mydb');
$rval = mysql_query( $sql, $con );
if(! $rval )
{
die('Failed to enter data: ' . mysql_error());
}
echo "The data was successfully entered into the database\n";
mysql_close($con);
?>
```

Once you have written the program, just run it. Open the MySQL command prompt and check whether the data has been successfully inserted into the database.

The following are the contents of my table:

student_id	student_name	student_address	student_age	join_date
1	john	HJK	13	2015-05-06 16:30:57.000000

The above figure clearly shows that the data was successfully inserted into my database. The figure shows the contents of the table *"students"* in *"PhpMyAdmin"*. This comes installed with WampServer.

However, most web applications do not function like this. Under normal circumstances, the data to be entered into the database is usually fetched from an HTML form. This means that users will have the choice of entering data that they wish. Users are also not allowed to access the PHP code of your web application. Let us demonstrate how to do this with an example:

Just write the following program and run it:

<html>

<head>

<title>Add a record from an HTML form</title>

```php
</head>
<body>
<?php
if(isset($_POST['add']))
{
$dbhost = 'localhost:3036';
$dbuser = 'root';
$dbpass = '';
$con = mysql_connect($dbhost, $dbuser, $dbpass);
if(! $con )
{
die('Failed to connect: ' . mysql_error());
}
if(! get_magic_quotes_gpc() )
{
$student_name = addslashes
($_POST['student_name']);
$student_address = addslashes
($_POST['student_address']);
}
else
{
$student_name = $_POST['student_name'];
$student_address = $_POST['student_address'];
}
```

```php
$student_age = $_POST['student_age'];

$sql = "INSERT INTO students ".
"( student_name,student_address, student_age,
join_date) ".
"VALUES('$
student_name,$student_address,$student_age,
NOW())";
mysql_select_db('mydb');
$rval = mysql_query( $sql, $con );
if(! $rval )
{
die('Failed to enter the enter data: ' . mysql_error());
}
echo " The data was entered successfully\n";
mysql_close($con);
}
else
{
?>
<form method="post" action="<?php $_PHP_SELF
?>">
<table width="400" border="0" cellspacing="1"
cellpadding="2">
<tr>
```

```html
<td width="Student Name</td>
<td><input name="student_name" type="text"
id="student_name"></td>
</tr>
<tr>
<td width="100">Student Address</td>
<td><input name="student_address" type="text"
id="student_address"></td>
</tr>
<tr>
<td width="100">Student age</td>
<td><input name="student_age" type="text"
id="student_age"></td>
</tr>
<tr>
<td width="100"> </td>
<td> </td>
</tr>
<tr>
<td width="100"> </td>
<td>
<input name="add" type="submit" id="add"
value="Add student">
</td>
</tr>
```

```
</table>
</form>
<?php
}
?>
</body>
</html>
```

Just save the program and then open it in your browser. You will observe the following output:

Student Name   [   ]

Student
Address   [   ]

Student age   [   ]

[Add student]

Just provide the details in the given fields of the output. As an example, I have provided the following data in my form:

Student Name	victor
Student Address	TYT
Student age	14

[Add student]

After inserting your own data, click on the *"Add student"* button. Open the MySQL command prompt and check to be sure that the data has been added to the database.

My database table now contains the following contents:

student_id	student_name	student_address	student_age	join_date
1	john	HJK	13	2015-05-06 16:30:57.000000
2	victor	TYT	14	2015-05-06 17:04:10.000000

The figure clearly shows that the new student was successfully added to my database. Employing PHP to update your database from an HTML form is that simple.

Notice the use of the function *"get_magic_quotes_gpc()"* to check whether the current configuration for magic quote has been set or not. If the above function returns false, we then use the function *"addslashes()"* so as to add slashes before the quotes.

Retrieving Data from a Database

Sometimes, you might need to know the data now contained in your database. This data should be shown on some specified text fields or a table. One only needs to set the *"SELECT"* statement and then execute it using the *"mysql_query()"* function. However, most PHP developers use the method *"mysql_fetch_array()"*, which returns the rows of data from the database table as an associative array, a numeric array, or a combination of the two.

Consider the following example:

```php
<?php
$dbhost = 'localhost:3036';
$dbuser = 'root';
$dbpass = '';
$conn = mysql_connect($dbhost, $dbuser, $dbpass);
if(! $con )
{
die('Failed to connect: ' . mysql_error());
```

```php
        }
$sql = 'SELECT student_name,student_address,
        student_age FROM students';

        mysql_select_db('mydb');
$rval = mysql_query( $sql, $con );
                if(! $rval )
                {
die('Failed to get data: ' . mysql_error());
                }
while($row = mysql_fetch_array($rval,
        MYSQL_ASSOC))
                {
echo "student_id:{$row['student_id']}  <br> ".
"student_name : {$row['student_name']} <br> ".
"student_age : {$row['student_age']} <br> ".
    "------------------------------<br>";
                }
echo "Data was fetched successfully\n";
        mysql_close($con);
                ?>
```

Run the program and observe the output. The code should output the table together with the details. Using the examples from my system, I get the following output:

student_id	student_name	student_address	student_age	join_date
1	john	HJK	13	2015-05-06 16:30:57.000000
2	victor	TYT	14	2015-05-06 17:04:10.000000

Here is an alternative method to achieve the same result in PHP:

```php
<?php
$dbhost = 'localhost:3036';
$dbuser = 'root';
$dbpass = '';
$con = mysql_connect($dbhost, $dbuser, $dbpass);
if(! $con )
{
die('Failed to connect: ' . mysql_error());
}
$sql = ' SELECT student_name,student_address,
student_age FROM students';

mysql_select_db('mydb');
$rval = mysql_query( $sql, $con );
```

```php
if(! $rval )
{
die('Failed to get data: ' . mysql_error());
}
while($row = mysql_fetch_array($rval, MYSQL_NUM))
{
echo "student_id :{$row[0]} <br> ".
"student_name : {$row[1]} <br> ".
"student_age : {$row[2]} <br> ".
"--------------------------------<br>";
}
echo "Data was fetched successfully\n";
mysql_close($con);
?>
```

Again, run the program and observe the result. On my system, it gives the following output:

student_id	student_name	student_address	student_age	join_date
1	john	HJK	13	2015-05-06 16:30:57.000000
2	victor	TYT	14	2015-05-06 17:04:10.000000

The resulting output is the same as the one we got using the first program.

Storing Images

Some people like to store their images uploaded into a folder on their server. Because image files contain binary data, however, if we us a data type called "BLOb" (Binary Large Object) for the purpose of storing the image it is possible to do so in your MySQL database. Let us create a new table in the same database, this time calling it *"mydb"*:

```php
<?php
$con = mysql_connect ("localhost","root","");
if (!$con)
{
die ('Failed to connect: ' . mysql_error());
}
mysql_select_db ("newdb", $con);
$sql = "CREATE TABLE images(Id INT PRIMARY KEY AUTO_INCREMENT, image MEDIUMBLOB)";
mysql_query($sql,$con);
echo "The Table was Created successfully!!";
mysql_close($con);
?>
```

Run the sequence of code above. It is generally a good to verify that the table has been formed properly. Next, run the following command on the MySQL command prompt:

```
mysql> show tables;
+------------------+
| Tables_in_mydb   |
+------------------+
| images           |
| students         |
+------------------+
2 rows in set (0.00 sec)

mysql>
```

The figure above shows that the table was created successfully. Now, let us confirm that the table has the right attributes:

```
mysql> desc images;
+-------+------------+------+-----+---------+----------------+
| Field | Type       | Null | Key | Default | Extra          |
+-------+------------+------+-----+---------+----------------+
| Id    | int(11)    | NO   | PRI | NULL    | auto_increment |
| image | mediumblob | YES  |     | NULL    |                |
+-------+------------+------+-----+---------+----------------+
2 rows in set (0.03 sec)

mysql>
```

From the above figure you can see that the table has two attributes which we specified. Notice that a single database can have more than one tables in MySQL. It is also possible to give similar names to tables in different databases.

Now we write the code to insert the image data into the database using the code as follows:

```php
<?php
$host = "localhost";
$user = "root";
$pass = "*";
$db = "mydb";
$cr = mysql_connect($host, $user, $pass);
if (!$cr) {
echo "Failed to connect to the server\n";
trigger_error(mysql_error(), E_USER_ERROR);
} else {
echo "Connection has been established\n";
}
$cr2 = mysql_select_db($mydb);
if (!$cr2) {
echo "failed to select the database\n";
```

```php
        trigger_error(mysql_error(), E_USER_ERROR);
    } else {
        echo "Database was selected successfully\n";
    }

    $file = "img.jpg";
    $imag = fopen($file, 'cr');
    if (!$imag) {
        echo "Failed to open the file for writing\n";
        trigger_error("Failed to open the file for writing \n",
            E_USER_ERROR);
    }

    $dt = fread($imag, filesize($file));
    if (!$dt) {
        echo "Failed to read image data\n";
        trigger_error("Failed to read image data\n",
            E_USER_ERROR);
    }

    $sdata = mysql_real_escape_string($dt);
    fclose($imag);
```

```php
$query = "INSERT INTO images(Id, image) Values(1,
'$sdata')";

$r = mysql_query($query);

if (!$r) {

echo "Failed to execute the query: $query";

trigger_error(mysql_error(), E_USER_ERROR);

} else {

echo "The Query was successfully executed\n";

}

mysql_close();

?>
```

The image file should be saved in the same directory as the above script and has been read in the following line of code:

```php
$file = "img.jpg";
```

The use of the *"fread()"* function means that after the image has been read, the result will be a string of data. To avoid the appearance of characters which are not safe for use in a SQL query, we have used the following method:

$sdata = mysql_real_escape_string($dt);

The above method will make your database more secure. We can then check to confirm whether or not the image was inserted into the database:

```
mysql> select * from images;
+------+-----------+
| Id   | image     |
+------+-----------+
|   1  | img.jpg   |
+------+-----------+
1 row in set (0.00 sec)

mysql>
```

The output from the database as in this figure shows that the image was inserted into the database successfully. You now know how to save image into your database.

Reading Images

Since you know how to write an image into the database, it's time to learn how to read it from the database table using following piece of PHP code:

```php
<?php
$host = "localhost";
$user = "root";
$pass = "";
$db = "mydb";
$rs = mysql_connect($host, $user, $pass);
if (!$rs) {
echo "Failed to connect to the server\n";
trigger_error(mysql_error(), E_USER_ERROR);
} else {
echo "Connection has been established\n";
}
```

```php
$rs2 = mysql_select_db($db);

if (!$rs2) {

echo "Failed to select the database\n";

trigger_error(mysql_error(), E_USER_ERROR);

} else {

echo "The Database was selectedsuccessfully\n";

}

$query = "SELECT image FROM images WHERE Id=1";

$rc = mysql_query($query);

if (!$rc) {

echo "Failed to execute the query: $query";

trigger_error(mysql_error(), E_USER_ERROR);

} else {

echo "The query: $query was executed successfully\n";

}

$row = mysql_fetch_row($rc);

$file = "woman2.jpg";

$imag = fopen($file, 'wb');

if (!$imag) {
```

```php
        echo "Failed to open the file for writing\n";
        trigger_error("Cannot open file for writing\n",
            E_USER_ERROR);
    }

    $rs3 = fwrite($imag, $row[0]);
    if (!$rs3) {
        echo "Failed to write the image to file\n";
        trigger_error("Failed to write the image to file\n",
            E_USER_ERROR);
    }

    fclose($imag);
    mysql_close();
?>
```

Just write the above program, save and then run it. If you have saved a JPEG file in the database in our first program, then this program should read and output it for you. In my case, I get the following result from running the program:

The output shows that my program ran successfully. The figure shows the image which I had originally saved into the database now retrieved to the browser. While developing web applications, for example, for a school you might need to use the pictures of students in the app. You can make use of this program to achieve this. Compared to the alternative method where the image is uploaded to a folder on the server side, this method is simple and can be done much more easily. It is recommended that you use this method.

What we have done is read a single image from our database table using the following line of code:

$query = "SELECT Data FROM images WHERE Id=1";

We have then fetched that single row contained in the database with the following code:

$row = mysql_fetch_row($rs);

This is the row with the image:

$file = "img.jpg";

The image has been opened as a binary code, and a writable one. This is for the sake of comparison. We need to be sure that the image we get is the one we had inserted into the database. The *"fwrite()"* will write the data to the file system.

Releasing Memory

It is highly recommended that after each *"SELECT"* statement, the cursor memory should be released. To do this, we use the function *"mysql_free_result()"*. Consider the example shown below:

```php
<?php
$dbhost = 'localhost:3036';
$dbuser = 'root';
$dbpass = '';
$con = mysql_connect($dbhost, $dbuser, $dbpass);
if(! $con )
{
die('Failed to connect: ' . mysql_error());
}
$sql = ' SELECT student_name,student_address,
student_age FROM students';
mysql_select_db('mydb');
$rval = mysql_query( $sql, $con );
if(! $rval )
{
die('Failed to get data: ' . mysql_error());
```

```php
        }
while($row = mysql_fetch_array($rval, MYSQL_NUM))
        {
        echo "STUDENT ID :{$row[0]}  <br> ".
        "STUDENT NAME : {$row[1]} <br> ".
        " STUDENT AGE : {$row[2]} <br> ".
        "-------------------------------<br>";
        }
        mysql_free_result($rval);
        echo "Data was fetched successfully\n";
        mysql_close($con);
        ?>
```

Paging

It is possible that your database may contain millions of records. In this situation it's possible that all of the records will not fit onto a single page. If you tried to select all of these records from your database with PHP at the same time, a problem would occur when you attempted to display them on your web page.

With PHP, however, you can use the "*LIMIT*" clause to paginate the output. This clause takes only two arguments. The first argument is the "*OFFSET*" and the second argument specifies the number of records to be fetched from the database.

Consider the example given below:

```
<html>
<head>
<title>Pagination in PHP</title>
</head>
<body>
```

```php
<?php
$dbhost = 'localhost:3036';
$dbuser = 'root';
$dbpass = '';
$rec_limit = 8;
$con = mysql_connect($dbhost, $dbuser, $dbpass);
if(! $con )
{
die('Failed to connect: ' . mysql_error());
}
mysql_select_db('mydb');
/* obtaining the total number of records */
$sql = "SELECT count(student_id) FROM student ";
$rval = mysql_query( $sql, $con );
if(! $rval )
{
die('Failed to get the data: ' . mysql_error());
}
$row = mysql_fetch_array($rval, MYSQL_NUM );
$rec_count = $row[0];

if( isset($_GET{'page'} ) )
{
$page = $_GET{'page'} + 1;
$offset = $rec_limit * $page ;
```

```php
        }
    else
        {
        $page = 0;
        $offset = 0;
        }
    $left_rec = $rec_count - ($page * $rec_limit);


$sql = " SELECT student_name,student_address,
            student_age ".
        "FROM students ".
        "LIMIT $offset, $rec_limit";
        $rval = mysql_query( $sql, $con );
            if(! $rval )
            {
die('Failed to get the data: ' . mysql_error());
            }
        while($row = mysql_fetch_array($rval,
            MYSQL_ASSOC))
            {
echo "STUDENT ID :{$row['student_id']}  <br> ".
"STUDENT NAME : {$row['student_name']} <br> ".
"STUDENT AGE : {$row['student_age']} <br> ".
        "--------------------------------<br>";
            }
```

```php
if( $page > 0 )
{
   $last = $page - 2;
   echo "<a href=\"$_PHP_SELF?page=$last\">The last 8
Records</a> |";
   echo "<a href=\"$_PHP_SELF?page=$page\">The next
8 Records</a>";
}
else if( $page == 0 )
{
   echo "<a href=\"$_PHP_SELF?page=$page\">The next
8 Records</a>";
}
else if( $left_rec < $rec_limit )
{
   $last = $page - 2;
   echo "<a href=\"$_PHP_SELF?page=$last\">The last 8
Records</a>";
}
mysql_close($con);
?>
```

Updating Data

Once you have your data in the database, you might need to alter something in it. This may be a whole record or it may be only a part of it. This can easily be done with PHP. Using the *"mysql_query()"* function let us write a statement which will perform this task.

Use the following as an example

```
<html>
<head>
<title>Updating the contents of MySQL database</title>
</head>
<body>

<?php
if(isset($_POST['update']))
{
$dbhost = 'localhost:3036';
$dbuser = 'root';
$dbpass = '';
```

```php
$con = mysql_connect($dbhost, $dbuser, $dbpass);
if(! $con )
{
die('Failed to connect: ' . mysql_error());
}
$student_id = $_POST['student_id'];
$student_age = $_POST['student_age];
$sql = "UPDATE students ".
"SET student_age = $student_age ".
"WHERE student_id = $student_id" ;

mysql_select_db('mydb');
$rval = mysql_query( $sql, $con );
if(! $rval )
{
die('Failed to update data: ' . mysql_error());
}
echo "Data was updated successfully\n";
mysql_close($con);
}
else
{
?>
<form method="post" action="<?php $_PHP_SELF ?>">
```

```html
<table width="400" border="0" cellspacing="1"
cellpadding="2">
<tr>
<td width="100">Student ID</td>
<td><input name="student_id" type="text"
id="student_id"></td>
</tr>
<tr>
<td width="100">Student Age</td>
<td><input name="student_age" type="text"
id="student_age"></td>
</tr>
<tr>
<td width="100"> </td>
<td> </td>
</tr>
<tr>
<td width="100"> </td>
<td>
<input name="update" type="submit" id="update"
value="Update Record">
</td>
</tr>
</table>
</form>
```

```php
<?php
}
?>
</body>
</html>
```

Deleting Data

It is possible to delete data contained in a MySQL database table. You just have to create the delete statement and then execute it using the *"mysql_execute()"* function. Just as we did while altering data, we must begin by matching the clause to be deleted.

Consider the following example:

```
<html>
<head>
<title>Delete a MySQL database record</title>
</head>
<body>
<?php
if(isset($_POST['delete']))
{
$dbhost = 'localhost:3036';
$dbuser = 'root';
$dbpass = '';
$con = mysql_connect($dbhost, $dbuser, $dbpass);
if(! $con )
```

```php
    {
        die('Failed to connect: ' . mysql_error());
    }
    $student_id = $_POST['student_id'];
    $sql = "DELETE student ".
    "WHERE student_id = $student_id" ;

    mysql_select_db('mydb');
    $rval = mysql_query( $sql, $con );
    if(! $rval )
    {
        die('Failed to delete the data delete data: ' .
        mysql_error());
    }
    echo "The data was deleted successfully\n";
    mysql_close($con);
}
else
{
?>
<form method="post" action="<?php $_PHP_SELF
?>">
<table width="400" border="0" cellspacing="1"
cellpadding="2">
<tr>
```

```html
<td width="100">Student ID</td>
<td><input name="student_id" type="text"
id="student_id"></td>
</tr>
<tr>
<td width="100"> </td>
<td> </td>
</tr>
<tr>
<td width="100"> </td>
<td>
<input name="delete" type="submit" id="delete"
value="Delete Record">
</td>
</tr>
</table>
</form>
<?php
}
?>
</body>
</html>
```

After running the above program, you will get the following output:

Student ID   [   ]

                        [Delete Record]

Just specify the *"ID"* of the student that you want to delete. I will specify the ID of *"2"* as an example from my own database. After this, click on the *"Delete Record"* button. In my case, the above ID is for a student named *"Victor"*. The above procedure should then delete this student from my database.

After checking the contents of my table, I get the following result:

student_id	student_name	student_address	student_age	join_date
1	john	HJK	13	2015-05-06 16:30:57.000000

This clearly shows that the student named *"Victor"* was deleted from the database.

Backing up the Database

As a precaution in case some sort of error occurs, it is highly recommended that you perform frequent backups of your database. This can be done in three the following three different ways:

- SQL Command through PHP.

- MySQL binary mysqldump through PHP.

- phpMyAdmin user interface.

Let us discuss how this can be done with the SQL command line through PHP.

To perform a backup of a table, you only need to execute the *"SQL SELECT"* command. If you need to back up the whole database, however, you have to backup each table using separate commands. Consider the following example:

```php
<?php
$dbhost = 'localhost:3036';
$dbuser = 'root';
$dbpass = '';
$con = mysql_connect($dbhost, $dbuser, $dbpass);
if(! $con )
{
die('Failed to connect: ' . mysql_error());
}
$table_name = "students";
$backup_file  = "/tmp/students.sql";
$sql = "SELECT * INTO OUTFILE '$backup_file' FROM $table_name";
mysql_select_db('mydb');
$rval = mysql_query( $sql, $con );
```

```php
if(! $rval )

{

die('Failed to back up the data: ' . mysql_error());

}

echo "Data was Backedup  successfully\n";

mysql_close($con);

?>
```

You might also need to restore some data which you had previously backed up from your database. This is simple matter of running the "*LOAD DATA INFILE*" command.

This is demonstrated in the following example:

```php
<?php
$dbhost = 'localhost:3036';
$dbuser = 'root';
$dbpass = '';
$con = mysql_connect($dbhost, $dbuser, $dbpass);
if(! $con )
{
die('Failed to connect: ' . mysql_error());
}
$table_name = "students";
$backup_file  = "/tmp/students.sql";
$sql = "LOAD DATA INFILE '$backup_file' INTO TABLE $table_name";
```

```php
mysql_select_db('mydb');

$rval = mysql_query( $sql, $con );

if(! $rval )

{

die('Failed to load data : ' . mysql_error());

}

echo "Data was loaded  successfully\n";

mysql_close($con);

?>
```

MySQL binary provides a utility called "mysqldump" that can be used to perform a database backup. Consider the following code:

```php
<?php
$dbhost = 'localhost:3036';
$dbuser = 'root';
$dbpass = '';


$backup_file = $dbname . date("Y-m-d-H-i-s") . '.gz';
$com = "mysqldump --opt -h $dbhost -u $dbuser -p $dbpass ".
"mydb | gzip > $backup_file";

system($com);
?>
```

Just run the above code in your machine. It will perform a complete backup on the database named "*mydb*".

If you have installed "*WampServer*" on your computer, you can use the "*PhpMyAdmin*" interface to perform a backup of your database. Open the interface and in its main page, click on the link labeled "*Export*".

The link is visible in the figure shown above. Just click on it and you will be prompted to select the database to be backed-up. This will automatically backup the database for you. This is the easiest way to perform a database backup in MySQL.

Inserting Data from Radio Buttons

Most people use radio buttons to represent different values. In most cases, the options represented using the radio buttons are mutually exclusive, meaning that they cannot be selected at once. One has to choose one radio button among all the options. In our previous sections, you learned how to insert data from a text box into MySQL database. Now, let us see how to display the value of a radio button in your database. Begin by creating a new database and a new table:

Use then following code to create a new database:

```php
<?php
$con = mysql_connect("localhost","root","");
if (!$con)
  {
  die('Failed to connect: ' . mysql_error());
  }
if (mysql_query("CREATE DATABASE newdb",$con))
  {
  echo "The Database was created !!";
  }
else
  {
  echo "Failed to create database: " . mysql_error();
  }
mysql_close($con);
?>
```

Just run the above code and it will create a new database for you. After that, check to confirm that the database has been properly formed. This can be done by opening the MySQL command prompt and running the following query:

show databases

In my case, I have the following output:

```
mysql> show databases;
+--------------------+
| Database           |
+--------------------+
| information_schema |
| db                 |
| mydb               |
| mysql              |
| newdb              |
| performance_schema |
| test               |
+--------------------+
7 rows in set (0.00 sec)

mysql>
```

The figure clearly shows that the database was, in fact, formed. Since we have a new database we now need to create a new table. Run the following piece of code:

```php
<?php
$con = mysql_connect ("localhost","root","");
if (!$con)
{
die ('Failed to connect: ' . mysql_error());
}
mysql_select_db ("newdb", $con);
$sql = "CREATE TABLE person
```

```
                (
       name VARCHAR( 60 ) ,
       sex VARCHAR( 60 ) ,
                )";
mysql_query($sql,$con);
echo "The Table was Created successfully!!";
mysql_close($con);
                ?>
```

Once the program is executed, confirm in the database to be sure that the table has output properly. This can be done by opening the MySQL command prompt and running the following commands:

➢ **use newdb**

➢ **show tables**

In my case, I receive the following output:

```
mysql> use newdb;
Database changed
mysql> show tables
    -> ;
+-------------------+
| Tables_in_newdb   |
+-------------------+
| person            |
+-------------------+
1 row in set (0.00 sec)

mysql>
```

To confirm whether my table has the correct attributes, I need to run the following command:

desc person

The above command gives the following result:

```
mysql> desc person;
+-------+-------------+------+-----+---------+-------+
| Field | Type        | Null | Key | Default | Extra |
+-------+-------------+------+-----+---------+-------+
| name  | varchar(60) | YES  |     | NULL    |       |
| sex   | varchar(60) | YES  |     | NULL    |       |
+-------+-------------+------+-----+---------+-------+
2 rows in set (0.02 sec)

mysql>
```

This shows that the table has the attributes that we have specified.

Now it is time to create the radio buttons and insert values for them. Just write the following code:

```php
<?php
$con = mysql_connect("localhost","root","");
mysql_select_db("newdb", $con);
@$n=$_POST['name'];
@$s=$_POST['sex'];
if(@$_POST['submit'])
{
echo $r="insert into person(name,sex)
values('$n','$s')";
echo "The data was Inserted successfully";
mysql_query($r);
}
?>
<html>
<body bgcolor="green">
<center>
<form method="post">
<table border="1" bgcolor="red">
<tr><td>Name</td>
<td><input type="text" name="name"/></td>
</tr>
<tr><td rowspan="2">Sex</td>
<td><input type="radio" name="sex"
value="Male"/>Male</td>
<tr>
```

```
<td><input type="radio" name="sex"
value="Female"/>Female</td></tr>
</tr>
<tr><td><input type="submit" name="submit"
value="Submit"/></td></tr>
</table>
</form>
</center>
</body>
</html>
```

Run the above program and observe the output. The following will be the result:

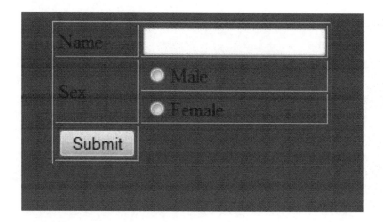

This is our HTML form which we have created with the above code. If

them to your favorite colors. Just enter your name and then choose the sex.

Personally, I will enter the following details:

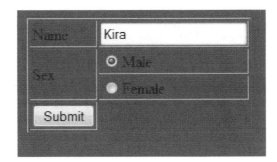

After doing that, just press the "*Submit*" button. This should send the data you have provided to the database as long as your code has no errors. At this point it is good to confirm that the insertion was successful. Open the table and check that its contents have updated.

This should be done by running the following command:

select * from person

In my case, the above command returns the following:

```
mysql> select * from person;
+--------+--------+
| name   | sex    |
+--------+--------+
| Kira   | Male   |
+--------+--------+
1 row in set (0.00 sec)

mysql>
```

This shows that the insertion was successful. We can go ahead and test it for the second time by providing some different details and then clicking on the *"Submit"* button. In my case, I will provide the following details:

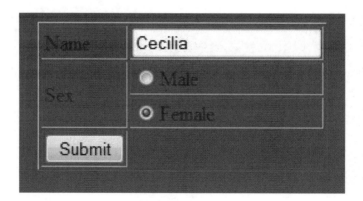

After providing your details, just hit the *"Submit"* button. Again, open your database and confirm that the insertion took place. In my case, I get the following result after the confirmation:

```
mysql> select * from person;
+----------+--------+
| name     | sex    |
+----------+--------+
| Kira     | Male   |
| Cecilia  | Female |
+----------+--------+
2 rows in set (0.00 sec)

mysql>
```

The figure clearly shows that again the insertion took place successfully.

Inserting Data from Check Boxes

Now that you know how to insert data into MySQL database from radio buttons and text boxes, what about when the data is in the form of check boxes? This is what we are going to tackle in this section. Check boxes are not intended to be mutually exclusive.

This means that one can insert multiple values into the database at a single go. Although you may wonder where you can use this feature, it might assist you some day. We will repeat the same procedure we had in radio button section.

Let us begin by creating a new database. Use the following code:

```php
<?php
$con = mysql_connect("localhost","root","");
if (!$con)
{
die('Failed to connect: ' . mysql_error());
}
if (mysql_query("CREATE DATABASE
checkboxdb",$con))
{
echo "The Database was created !!";
}
else
{
echo "Failed to create database: " . mysql_error();
}
mysql_close($con);
?>
```

It is good to confirm whether the database was formed. Just open the MySQL command prompt and run the following command:

show databases;

The command gives the following on my system:

```
mysql> show databases;
+--------------------+
| Database           |
+--------------------+
| information_schema |
| checkboxdb         |
| db                 |
| mydb               |
| mysql              |
| newdb              |
| performance_schema |
| test               |
+--------------------+
8 rows in set (0.00 sec)

mysql>
```

This is an indication that the database was successfully formed. We then need to create a new table in the new database. This can be done using the following code:

```php
<?php
$con = mysql_connect ("localhost","root","");
if (!$con)
{
die ('Failed to connect: ' . mysql_error());
}
mysql_select_db ("checkboxdb", $con);
$sql = "CREATE TABLE person
(
name VARCHAR( 60 ) ,
)";
mysql_query($sql,$con);
echo "The Table was Created successfully!!";
mysql_close($con);
?>
```

Notice that we have created a table named *"person"* in the
database *"checkboxdb"*. The table has only one attribute
(column), that is, *"name"*. It is good to confirm this so as to be
sure that the table has been properly formed. In my case, I have
the following:

```
mysql> use checkboxdb;
Database changed
mysql> show tables;
+------------------------+
| Tables_in_checkboxdb   |
+------------------------+
| person                 |
+------------------------+
1 row in set (0.00 sec)

mysql>
```

The next step is to check on the attributes of the table so as to be sure that they are correct. This should be done as follows:

```
mysql> desc person;
+-------+-------------+------+-----+---------+-------+
| Field | Type        | Null | Key | Default | Extra |
+-------+-------------+------+-----+---------+-------+
| name  | varchar(60) | YES  |     | NULL    |       |
+-------+-------------+------+-----+---------+-------+
1 row in set (0.07 sec)

mysql>
```

From the figure, it is clear that the table has a single attribute which is exactly what we specified in our PHP code.

We then need to create a PHP program that will connect the *"checkboxdb"* database to our PHP files. This should be as follows:

```php
<?php
$dbhost = 'localhost:3036';
$dbuser = 'root';
$dbpass = '';
$dbname= 'checkboxdb'
$con = mysql_connect($dbhost, $dbuser, $dbpass);
mysql_select_db('$dbname',$con);
?>
```

Give the file the name *"dbcon.php"*.

We then need to create the HTML form with the check boxes. This can be accomplished with the following code:

```html
<html>

<body>
```

```html
<form method="post" action="check.php">
<input type="checkbox" name="c1[]" value="Kira Life"> Kira Life <br />
<input type="checkbox" name="c1[]" value="Nicholas Samuel"> Nicholas Samuel<br />
<input type="checkbox" name="c1[]" value="Bismack Samuel"> Bismack Samuel <br />
<input type="checkbox" name="c1[]" value="Mercy John"> Mercy John <br />
<input type="checkbox" name="c1[]" value="Millicent Victor"> Millicent Victor <br />
<input type="submit" name="submit" value="submit">
</form>
</body>
</html>
```

Give the above form the name *"form.php"*.

Finally, we have to come up with a PHP script to insert the data from the check box into the database. The script should be as follows:

```php
<?php
include(dbcon.php')
$check = $_['c1'];
if($_POST["submit"]=="submit")
{
for ($j=0;$j<c1(sizeof($c1);$i++){
$query="INSERT INTO PERSON(name) values ('
".$c1[$j]."')";
Mysql_query($query) or die (mysql_error());
}
echo "values were inserted successfully";
}
?>
```

Your program is now ready to be run. You will observe the following after running the program:

☐ Kira Life
☐ Nicholas Samuel
☐ Bismack Samuel
☐ Mercy John
☐ Millicent Victor

[submit]

The output is the form which we created. It contains the check boxes together with their associated names. It isn't necessary to check all the buttons and you should note that the buttons are not mutually exclusive. You can select as many or as few as you like. In my case, I will choose the following names:

☑ Kira Life
☑ Nicholas Samuel
☐ Bismack Samuel
☑ Mercy John
☐ Millicent Victor

[submit]

Notice that I have selected only three names, but you can choose 2 or 4 names, it is does not matter. Once you are done, click on the *"submit"* button. This should insert the names that you have chosen into the database table. You need to check from the database to be sure that this has happened. In my case, I get the following result after querying my database:

This shows that the values were inserted successfully. This is a great step. You now know how to insert from a text box, radio buttons, check boxes and also directly using a PHP code.

Inserting Multiple Records

With PHP, it is possible to insert multiple records into the database at once. To achieve this, one must use the *"mysqli_multi_query()"* function. Consider the following examples which add new records to the table *"students"* which we created earlier:

```php
<?php
$servername = "localhost";
$username = "username";
$password = "";
$dbname = "mydb";
// establish a connection
$con = new mysqli($servername, $username,
$password, $dbname);
// Checking the status of the connection
if ($con->connect_error) {
die("Failed to connect: " . $con->connect_error);
}
$sql = "INSERT INTO students (student_name,
student_addres, student_age, join_date)
```

```php
        VALUES ('John', 'YUT', 12, NOW());";
$sql .= "INSERT INTO students (student_name,
    student_addres, student_age, join_date)
        VALUES ('Mary', 'TGH', 14, NOW() );";
$sql .= "INSERT INTO students (student_name,
    student_addres, student_age, join_date)
        VALUES ('Julie', HJY, 13,NOW())";
if ($con->multi_query($sql) === TRUE) {
echo "The new records were successfully created";
                } else {
    echo "Error: " . $sql . "<br>" . $con->error;
                }
            $con->close();
                ?>
```

Just write the above program and run it. Check to see whether the new records have inserted into the database table. In my case, I get the following result after querying the database:

student_id	student_name	student_address	student_age	join_date
1	john	HJK	13	2015-05-06 16:30:57.000000
3	John	YUT	12	2015-05-07 22:57:59.000000
4	Mary	TGH	14	2015-05-07 22:58:58.000000
5	Julie	HJY	13	2015-05-07 23:00:09.000000

From the above figure, it is very clear that the new records have been inserted into the database. That is the simplest way to insert multiple records simultaneously in a database. In the above example, the insertion has been done by employing the use of the object-oriented method.

To use this procedural method, it should be done as follows:

```php
<?php
$servername = "localhost";
$username = "username";
$password = "";
$dbname = "mydb";

// establish the connection
$con = mysql_connect($servername, $username,
$password, $dbname);
// Checking the status of the connection
if (!$con) {
die("Failed to connect: " . mysql_connect_error());
}
$sql = "INSERT INTO students (student_name,
student_addres, student_age, join_date)
VALUES ('John', 'YUT', 12, NOW());";
$sql .= "INSERT INTO students (student_name,
student_addres, student_age, join_date)
VALUES ('Mary', 'TGH', 14, NOW() );";
$sql .= "INSERT INTO students (student_name,
student_addres, student_age, join_date)
VALUES ('Julie', HJY, 13,NOW())";
```

```php
if (mysql_multi_query($con, $sql)) {
echo "New records created successfully";
} else {
echo "Error: " . $sql . "<br>" . mysql_error($con);
}
mysql_close($con);
?>
```

That is how it is done procedurally. However, the difference is not too great; the two programs will give you the same result when executed. Choose the method which you find yourself more comfortable with.

We can also use the PDO function to achieve the same result. This can be done as follows:

```php
<?php
$servername = "localhost";
$username = "username";
$password = "";
$dbname = "mydb";
try {
$conn = new
PDO("mysql:host=$servername;dbname=$dbname",
$username, $password);
// set the exception after occurrence of a PDO error
$con->setAttribute(PDO::ATTR_ERRMODE,
PDO::ERRMODE_EXCEPTION);
// start processing the transaction
$con->startTransaction();
// The SQL statements
$con = "INSERT INTO students (student_name,
student_addres, student_age, join_date)
VALUES ('John', 'YUT', 12, NOW());";
$con = "INSERT INTO students (student_name,
student_addres, student_age, join_date)
VALUES ('Mary', 'TGH', 14, NOW() );";
$con = "INSERT INTO students (student_name,
student_addres, student_age, join_date)
VALUES ('Julie', HJY, 13,NOW())";
// commit the above transaction
```

```php
        $con->commit();
        echo "New records were successfully inserted";
    }
    catch(PDOException $ex)
    {
        // in case something wrong happens, roll back the
        transaction
        $con->rollback();
        echo "Error: " . $ex->getMessage();
    }
    $con = null;
?>
```

Above is an example of a program which inserts multiple records simultaneously, done using PDO. Notice that this program is a bit different from the two other methods demonstrated above and a bit complex. However, any of these three methods can be used and the same result will be achieved. It all depends on what you want and the method that you find you are comfortable with or easier to work with. I can't tell you which one is best, you have to choose the best fit for yourself.

Using Prepared Statement

With prepared statements, programmers can efficiently execute MySQL statement(s) repeatedly. What happens is that an SQL statement is created and sent to the database where it is stored. Some of the parameters of this statement are left unspecified for flexibility purposes. It will then be possible for the programmer to provide different parameters for this statement at different times, meaning that they will not have to recreate the same statement every time you need it.

This makes the coding process much more efficient. The programmer or the application may execute this statement as many times as they need. Prepared statements are good since they safeguard your web applications and database from SQL injections.

The following example illustrate how prepared statements can be used in MySQL:

```php
<?php
$hostname = "localhost";
$username = "username";
$password = "";
$dbname = "mydb";

// Establish a connection
$con = new mysql($hostname, $username, $password, $dbname);
// Checking the status of the connection
if ($con->connect_error) {
die("Failed to connect: " . $con->connect_error);
}
// prepare and perform binding
$st = $con->prepare("INSERT INTO students (f student_name, student_addres, student_age, join_date) VALUES (?, ?, ?, ?)");
$st->bind_param("ssss", $student_name, $student_address, $student_age, $join_date);
// setting the parameters and then executing
$student_name = "Mathew";
$student_address = "DBK";
$student_age = "11";
$st->execute();
```

```php
$student_name = "Joel";
$student_address = "OPS";
$student_age = "15";
$st->execute();

$student_name = "Coggan";
$student_address = "KRN";
$student_age = "17";
$st->execute();
echo "The records were inserted successfully";
$st->close();
$con->close();
?>
```

Just write and run the above program. Check from the database to be sure that the new records have been created. After querying my database table, I get the following result:

student_id	student_name	student_address	student_age	join_date
1	john	HJK	13	2015-05-06 16:30:57.000000
3	John	YUT	12	2015-05-07 22:57:59.000000
4	Mary	TGH	14	2015-05-07 22:58:58.000000
5	Julie	HJY	13	2015-05-07 23:00:09.000000
6	Mathew	DBK	11	2015-05-08 00:09:38.000000
7	Joel	OPS	15	2015-05-08 00:10:15.000000
8	Coggan	KRN	17	2015-05-08 00:10:44.000000

From the figure above, it is clear that the three new records have been created. They form the last part of the *"students"* table.

Notice that we have only four parameters for the student. These four parameters are represented by the use of the "?" symbol four times in the following statement:

$st = $con->prepare("INSERT INTO students (student_name, student_address, student_age, join_date) VALUES (?, ?, ?, ?)");

This represents the parameters. Consider the following statement:

$st->bind_param("ssss", $student_name, $student_address, $student_age, $join_date);

Notice this section, *"ssss"*, which appears near the beginning of the statement above. *Each "s"* in this part of the statement represents a type of data for our parameters, and we have four parameters. The *"s"* shows that the parameter is of type *"string"*.

Parameters of other data types are represented as follows:

- **i - integer**
- **d - double**
- **b - BLOB**

Since we have specified the type of data that should be expected, we have avoided the risk of an SQL injection.

To achieve the same result using prepared statements in PDO, the code should be written as follows:

```php
<?php
$hostname = "localhost";
$username = "username";
$password = "";
$dbname = "mydb";
try {
$con = new
PDO("mysql:host=$hostname;dbname=$dbname",
$username, $password);
// setting the error mode to exception for PDO
$con->setAttribute(PDO::ATTR_ERRMODE,
PDO::ERRMODE_EXCEPTION);
// preparing the sql and binding the parameters
$st = $con->prepare("INSERT INTO students
(student_name, student_addres, student_age,
join_date)
VALUES (:student_name, : student_addres,
:student_age, :join_date)");
$st->bindParam(':student_name', $student_name);
$st->bindParam(':student_address',
$student_address);
$st->bindParam(':student_age', $student_age);
```

```php
$st->bindParam(':join_date', $join_date);
// inserting a new row
$student_name = "Mathew";
$student_address = "DBK";
$student_age = "11";
$st->execute();

//inserting a new row
$student_name = "Joel";
$student_address = "OPS";
$student_age = "15";
$st->execute();
```

```php
//inserting a new row
$student_name = "Coggan";
$student_address = "KRN";
$student_age = "17";
$st->execute();
echo "The records were inserted successfully";
}
catch(PDOException $ex)
{
echo "Error: " . $ex->getMessage();
}
$con = null;
?>
```

If you run the above program, the effect will be the same as the previous one. The difference is just a matter of how the problem is approached.

Transaction Processing

A transaction is made up of multiple operations which are all executed at the same time. Because the operations in a transaction either are or are not all executed it is said to be atomic or inseparable. If a single operation within the transaction fails, then the whole transaction is aborted. The transaction can be committed if and only if all of the operations in it are completed successfully. This feature is good for preventing the occurrence of some of the errors which might result in the database.

In MySQL, there are multiple data storage engines. InnoDB and MYISAM are the most commonly used in MySQL. By default, the MYISAM database storage engine is used in MySQL. This is due to the faster processing speed associated with them. However, they do not support transactions which explains the need for the InnoDB database storage engines. Although they are slow to process, they are good at protecting against loss of data and they also support transactions.

Consider the PHP code shown below:

```php
<?php
mysql_connect('localhost', 'root', '')
or die("Failed to connect to the database\n");
mysql_select_db("mydb") or die(mysql_error());
$rc1 = mysql_query("UPDATE Students SET Name =
'Mike' WHERE Id = 1")
or die(mysql_error());
$rc2 = mysql_query("UPDATE students SET Name =
'Ephraim' WHERE Id = 2")
or die(mysql_error());
$rc3 = mysql_query("UPDATE student SET Name =
'Jared' WHERE Id = 3")
or die(mysql_error());
mysql_close();
?>
```

Just write the above program. Save the file and then run it. In my case, I am using MYISAM as the storage engine for my database.

Our goal is to try to update the first three rows contained in the "*students*" table. Initially, the table has the following content:

student_id	student_name	student_address	student_age	join_date
1	john	HJK	13	2015-05-06 16:30:57.000000
3	John	YUT	12	2015-05-07 22:57:59.000000
4	Mary	TGH	14	2015-05-07 22:58:58.000000
5	Julie	HJY	13	2015-05-07 23:00:09.000000
6	Mathew	DBK	11	2015-05-08 00:09:38.000000
7	Joel	OPS	15	2015-05-08 00:10:15.000000
8	Coggan	KRN	17	2015-05-08 00:10:44.000000

Consider the following commands:

$rc1 = mysql_query("UPDATE Students SET Name = 'Mike' WHERE Id = 1")

or die(mysql_error());

$rc2 = mysql_query("UPDATE students SET Name = 'Ephraim' WHERE Id = 2")

or die(mysql_error());

What we are trying to do is to change the names contained in the first two rows. Consider this next statement as well:

$rc3 = mysql_query("UPDATE student SET Name = 'Jared' WHERE Id = 3")

or die(mysql_error());

These statements cannot be successfully executed. The reason is because the database does not contain a table named *"student"* which we have tried to select in these statements. After execution, this will result into an error.

However, on checking the contents of the table, I get the following:

student_id	student_name	student_address	student_age	join_date
1	Mike	HJK	13	2015-05-08 16:28:00.000000
3	Ephraim	YUT	12	2015-05-08 16:28:16.000000
4	Mary	TGH	14	2015-05-07 22:58:58.000000
5	Julie	HJY	13	2015-05-07 23:00:09.000000
6	Mathew	DBK	11	2015-05-08 00:09:38.000000
7	Joel	OPS	15	2015-05-08 00:10:15.000000
8	Coggan	KRN	17	2015-05-08 00:10:44.000000

From the above figure, it is very clear that the first two rows of the table were actually changed successfully while the third row did not change. This is the reason for the error we have discussed above. Avoiding errors such as these, in which a series of operations are only partially completed, is meant to be the advantage of using transaction.

In our case however, all the operations, changing the individual records in three different rows, were not successful. Due to the atomic nature of a transaction, however, this cannot be said to be a complete transaction and the whole transaction will then be rolled back so as to restore the database to its initial state.

Rolling back the transaction means that we should undo all the effects brought about by the transaction. This is what happens when you try to use transactions in MYISAM, which cannot execute them properly.

Let us recreate the *"students"* table but this time, the storage engine will be InnoDB. First, begin by dropping the table we had been using with the following:

```php
<?php
$dbhost = 'localhost:3036';
$dbuser = 'root';
$dbpass = '';
$con = mysql_connect($dbhost, $dbuser, $dbpass);
if(! $con )
{
die('Failed to connect: ' . mysql_error());
}
$sql = 'DROP TABLE students';
$rval = mysql_query( $sql, $con );
if(! $rval )
{
die('Failed to delete the table students: ' .
mysql_error());
}
echo "The table  was deleted successfully\n";
```

```php
mysql_close($con);
?>
```

Then, let us recreate the table:

```php
<?php
$dbhost = 'localhost:3036';
$dbuser = 'root';
$dbpass = '';
$con = mysql_connect($dbhost, $dbuser, $dbpass);
if(! $con )
{
die('Failed to connect: ' . mysql_error());
}
echo 'Connection was successful';
$sql = 'CREATE TABLE student(
'student_id INT NOT NULL AUTO_INCREMENT, '.
'student_name VARCHAR(20) NOT NULL, '.
'student_address  VARCHAR(20) NOT NULL, '.
'student_age   INT NOT NULL, '.
'join_date   timestamp(14) NOT NULL, '.
'primary key ( student_id ))'
'ENGINE=INNODB';
```

```php
mysql_select_db('mydb');
$rval = mysql_query( $sql, $con );
if(! $rval )
{
die('Failed to create the table: ' . mysql_error());
}
echo "Table student was created successfully\n";
mysql_close($con);
?>
```

Once again, confirm to be sure that the table has been formed. In my case, I get the following after the confirmation:

```
mysql> use mydb;
Database changed
mysql> show tables;
+------------------+
| Tables_in_mydb   |
+------------------+
| images           |
| students         |
+------------------+
2 rows in set (0.00 sec)

mysql>
```

From the above figure, it is very clear that the new table was formed successfully. If this is not the case, you can run the above program for a second time. Since the table is ready, let us populate it with some records which we will then try to change later.

This can be done with the following code:

```php
<?php
$servername = "localhost";
```

```php
$username = "username";
$password = "";
$dbname = "mydb";

// establish a connection
$con = new mysqli($servername, $username,
$password, $dbname);
// Checking the status of the connection
if ($con->connect_error) {
die("Failed to connect: " . $con->connect_error);
}
$sql = "INSERT INTO students (student_name,
student_addres, student_age, join_date)
VALUES ('Leonard', 'UIT', 12, NOW());";
$sql .= "INSERT INTO students (student_name,
student_addres, student_age, join_date)
VALUES ('Mary', 'TGH', 14, NOW() );";
$sql .= "INSERT INTO students (student_name,
student_addres, student_age, join_date)
VALUES ('Catherine', XYZ,13,NOW())";
if ($con->multi_query($sql) === TRUE) {
echo "The new records were successfully created";
} else {
echo "Error: " . $sql . "<br>" . $con->error;
}
```

```
$con->close();

?>
```

After the data insertion is executed, confirm that it was successfully completed. If this is not the case on your system, you can rerun the program. In my case, I get the following result:

Leonard	UIT	12	2015-05-08 16:56:30.000000
Mary	TGH	14	2015-05-08 16:57:15.000000
Catherine	XYZ	13	2015-05-08 16:58:08.000000

The above figure shows that the program ran successfully on my system.

Next write the following program:

```php
<?php
mysql_connect('localhost', 'root', '')
or die("Failed to connect to the database\n");
mysql_select_db("mydb") or die(mysql_error());
mysql_query("SET AUTOCOMMIT=0");
mysql_query("START TRANSACTION");
$rc1 = mysql_query("DELETE FROM students WHERE
Id = 3")
or die(mysql_error());

$rc2 = mysql_query("DELETE FROM students WHERE
Id = 4")
or die(mysql_error());
$rc3 = mysql_query("DELETE FROM student WHERE
Id = 5")
or die(mysql_error());
if ($rc1 and $rc2 and $rc3) {
mysql_query("COMMIT");
} else {
mysql_query("ROLLBACK");
}
mysql_close();
?>
```

In the above program, the third SQL statement has an error. In the database "*mydb*", we have a table named "*students*" with an "s", not "*student*" as we have specified in the third SQL statement of the program which is wrong.

The three SQL statements are intended to delete the three records which we have added to the newly created table. Just run the program. After this, open the table in order to confirm that the deletion took place or not. After querying my table, I get the following feedback:

Leonard	UIT	12	2015-05-08 16:56:30.000000
Mary	TGH	14	2015-05-08 16:57:15.000000
Catherine	XYZ	13	2015-05-08 16:58:08.000000

From the above figure, it is very clear that the deletion did not take place. The reason behind this is that an error occurred before executing the "*Commit*" statement. This is due to the error in the third SQL statement. This led to execution of the "*ROLLBACK*" statement, which returned the table to its original state. This clearly shows that in MySQL, a transaction is an atomic unit of work. Using InnoDB as the database storage engine is good as it supports transactions.

Conclusion

As you can see PHP is a programming language made to be used for the development of web applications. The language is mostly used to add functionality to an HTML interface. To connect a web application to a database, and especially MySQL database management system, or merely to add functionality to an HTML interface, then you simply must use PHP. It's the clear choice. The language offers greater flexibility as there are multiple ways to achieve a unit goal.

Because the process of connecting to a database requires a great deal of decision making, programs turn to PHP for its use and support of loops and decision making statements. It makes even simple tasks easier; you can use PHP to create a new MySQL database as well as to create a new table. Once these have been created, data can be populated into the table with PHP. That data can be specified in the PHP code and the respective columns of the table can be specified to hold each datum.

One can also choose to insert data from an HTML form, whereby the user is allowed to enter data in text boxes, radio buttons, check boxes, even images. All of these tasks and more are now at your fingertips, simply through the knowledge and use of the PHP language. The last step is to go out and start writing. Create your web application and feel secure and confident in your new found knowledge.

Thank you!

We would like to thank you for buying this book. Hope you found it helpful in your now EASY and FAST programming life development. And we are happy to recommend you some other books from this author:

1. ANDROID PROGRAMMING: Complete Introduction for Beginners -Step By Step Guide How to Create Your Own Android App Easy!

http://www.amazon.com/gp/product/B00WPK68IQ?*Version*=1&*entries*=0

2.   ANDROID GAME PROGRAMMING: COMPLETE INTRODUCTION FOR BEGINNERS: STEP BY STEP GUIDE HOW TO CREATE YOUR OWN ANDROID APP EASY!

http://www.amazon.com/gp/product/B011R2H2JQ?*Version*=1&*entries*=0

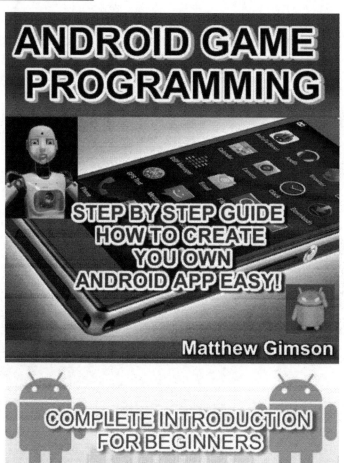

3. Linux Command Line: FAST and EASY! (Linux Commands, Bash Scripting Tricks, Linux Shell Programming Tips and Bash One-Liners)

http://www.amazon.com/gp/product/B00VPJ100Y?*Version*=1&*entries*=0

4. **Linux Command Line: Become a Linux Expert! (Input/Output Redirection, Wildcards, File Security, Processes Managing, Shell Programming Advanced Features, GUI elements, Useful Linux Commands)**

http://www.amazon.com/gp/product/B00 XGUO4E4?*Version*=1&*entries*=0

5. **Python Programming: Getting started FAST With Learning of Python Programming Basics in No Time.**

http://www.amazon.com/gp/product/B00W UNSH6Y?*Version*=1&*entries*=0

6. DOCKER: Everything You Need to Know to Master Docker (Docker Containers, Linking Containers, Whalesay Image, Docker Installing on Mac OS X and Windows OS)

http://www.amazon.com/gp/product/B013X2R PT0?*Version*=1&*entries*=0

7. Docker: Docker Guide for Production Environment (Programming is Easy Book 8)

http://www.amazon.com/gp/product/B01452V9
IA?*Version*=1&*entries*=0

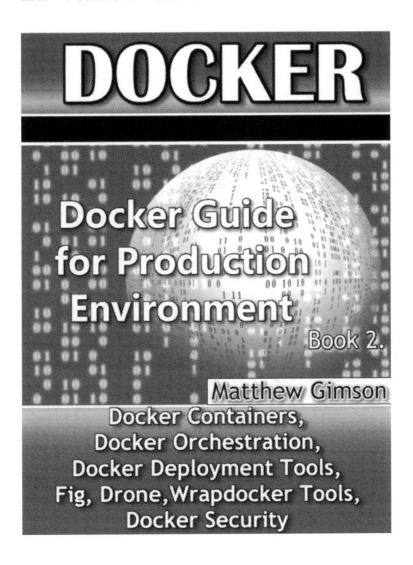

8. Excel VBA Programming: Learn Excel
VBA Programming FAST and EASY!
(Programming is Easy Book 9)

http://www.amazon.com/gp/product/Bo14DIP
GVW?*Version*=1&*entries*=0

9. VAGRANT: Make Your Life Easier With VAGRANT. Master VAGRANT FAST and EASY! (Programming is Easy Book 10)

http://www.amazon.com/gp/product/B0151GIR CA?*Version*=1&*entries*=0

10. SCALA PROGRAMMING: Learn Scala Programming FAST and EASY! (Programming is Easy Book 11)

http://www.amazon.com/gp/product/B0151TBXEQ?*Version*=1&*entries*=0

11. NODE. JS: Practical Guide for Beginners (Programming is Easy Book 12)

http://www.amazon.com/gp/product/B01588CXAS?*Version*=1&*entries*=0

12. IOS 8 APP DEVELOPMENT. Develop Your Own App FAST and EASY!

http://www.amazon.com/gp/product/B015CMEJVQ?*Version*=1&*entries*=0

Made in the USA
Lexington, KY
28 May 2016